A LITTLE
HISTORY
OF
IRELAND

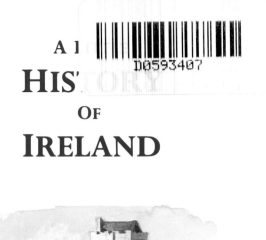

Martin Wallace

Illustrations by Ian McCullough

APPLETREE PRESS

First published in 1994 by
The Appletree Press Ltd
19–21 Alfred Street
Belfast BT2 8DL

British Library Cataloguing-in-Publication Data
A catalogue record for this book is available
from the British Library.

ISBN 0 86281 455 3

9 8 7 6 5 4 3 2 1

CONTENTS

SAINTS AND SCHOLARS

I rish history really begins with Saint Patrick, who converted Ireland to Christianity. The son of a civil servant in Roman Britain, he was abducted and sold into slavery in County Antrim. Escaping to the European mainland, he eventually returned to Ireland as a missionary and bishop. His first church was at Saul, in County Down, and he later made Armagh the ecclesiastical capital of the island, as it has remained. Traditionally his arrival in Ireland has been dated 432 AD, but some scholars believe it was much later in the fifth century and that he completed the work begun by an earlier missionary.

Whatever the truth of this, Christianity provided not merely a religion but also a written language, Latin. A tradition of storytelling had preserved accounts of great events, tribal histories and genealogies. Now there were scholars who recorded this material on vellum manuscripts, no doubt amending and embroidering it as they blended fact and legend. Such laborious work was aided by the spread of monasteries, often on isolated islands or mountains, where monks lived austerely and could pursue their studies free from the demands placed on conventional priests.

Ireland, situated at the western edge of Europe, was certainly inhabited as early as 6,000 BC. Archaeology provides evidence of successive invasions, hunters and fishermen followed by farmers using stone tools to clear land, then by tribes skilled in metalwork. The last pre-Christian invaders were the iron-using Celts or Gaels, who reached Ireland around 600 BC. More than 1,000 years later, it was a well-established pagan Celtic society which accepted Christianity.

Fifth-century Ireland was divided into a number of small kingdoms. The more influential kings received tribute from the weaker ones, but the idea of a high king of Ireland is a later invention. The Celts were cattle farmers, wealthy enough to devote some resources to intricate gold and silver ornaments, sophisticated enough to have lawyers (*brehons*) and poets (*filidh*) as well as the druids who practised magic and offered sacrifices to the pagan gods. They had their own language, from which modern Irish has evolved. Kings were elected, but from a narrowly defined group possessing royal blood. Wars were common, and the balance of power between kingdoms shifted constantly.

Saint Patrick divided Ireland into dioceses, but before long abbots became more influential than bishops. The monasteries were important seats of learning at a time when the European mainland was entering a dark age following the collapse of the Roman Empire. In time Irish monks set out to spread the Christian message in foreign countries. Among them were Saint Columba, who founded a famous monastery on the Scottish island of Iona, and Saint Columbanus, who founded monasteries in France, Germany and Italy.

Ireland had escaped invasion by the Roman legions, but it could not escape the Viking longboats which menaced its coasts and rivers in the ninth century. But, while the Norsemen sacked monasteries, they also settled as traders and founded settlements which grew into such cities as Dublin, Cork and Limerick. The Celtic kingdoms eventually fought back, and in 1014 Brian Boru, who had claimed the high kingship, won a decisive victory over the Norsemen at Clontarf, near Dublin.

By now the Church was in disarray, the monasteries corrupt and the dioceses ineffective. However, the establishment of Cistercian monasteries from 1142 on, and the reorganisation of the Irish Church at the Synod of Kells in 1152 set reforms in motion. The petty kingdoms remained a source of disunion. Brian Boru had been killed at Clontarf, and successive aspirants to the high kingship were unable to enforce their authority. The land of saints and scholars lacked military and political cohesion, and was in no condition to repel the next invaders who sailed for Ireland.

THE NORMAN CONQUEST

At the beginning of May 1169, three single-masted longships beached at Bannow Bay, County Wexford. They had sailed from Milfordhaven in Wales, and on board were Normans, Welshmen and Flemings. Their leader was Robert FitzStephen, a Welsh warlord, and they made camp on Bannow Island, separated from the mainland by a narrow channel which has since silted up. A day later, two further ships arrived under the command of Maurice de Prendergast, bringing their numbers to around 600. They were soon joined by 500 Irish warriors led by Dermot MacMurrough, King of Leinster. A century had passed since the Battle of Hastings, when William the Conqueror had launched the Norman invasion and systematic colonisation of England. Now the Norman conquest of Ireland had begun.

The invasion of 1169 sprang from the long-standing enmity of Dermot MacMurrough and Tiernan O'Rourke of Breifne, a more northerly kingdom. Dermot had once abducted Tiernan's wife Dervorgilla, and in 1166 Tiernan sought revenge. Dermot, forced out of his headquarters at Ferns, fled to England. He landed at Bristol, and eventually made his way to Aquitaine in France, where he appealed to Henry II for help. Although he was King of England, Henry was a French-speaking Norman much preoccupied with controlling his French territories. However, he had contemplated an invasion of Ireland as early as 1155, with the approval of the only English Pope, Adrian IV, and he readily authorised Dermot to seek allies among the Norman lords in Britain.

Returning to Bristol, Dermot was initially unsuccessful, so he turned his attention to Wales, where the Normans were perpetually engaged in warfare against the native Welsh. Richard FitzGilbert de Clare, Earl of Pembroke, proved an attentive listener. Pembroke, known as Strongbow, was an experienced campaigner, but he had fallen out of favour at Henry's court. Ireland offered an opportunity to restore his standing and add to his wealth, but he put a price on his assistance. He was to marry Dermot's daughter Aoife, and in time succeed to the kingship of Leinster. With Strongbow's approval, Dermot won the support of FitzStephen and other Welsh-Norman lords, to whom he promised grants of land. He returned to Ireland with a small army in 1167, but was defeated by his old enemy Tiernan O'Rourke and forced to pay one hundred ounces of gold in reparation for the abduction of Dervorgilla. Two years later, it would be a different story.

From Bannow the combined armies headed towards Wexford, a Norse seaport some twenty miles away. There was a brief skirmish at Duncormick, before the assault on Wexford's walls. After some resistance, the Norsemen acknowledged the superiority of the armoured knights and their archers and surrendered the town. A year later, in response to a plea from Dermot, Strongbow despatched a small force under Raymond le Gros. It landed at Baginbun, near Bannow, and immediately routed a strong army of Irishmen and Norsemen from Waterford, inspiring the couplet: "At the creek of Baginbun, Ireland was lost and won." Strongbow himself arrived with 1,200 men in August 1170, stormed Waterford, where he married Aoife MacMurrough, and within a month had captured Dublin.

With Dermot's death in May 1171, Strongbow became King of Leinster, and his skilful knights and archers continued to defeat larger Irish and Norse armies. The arrival of Henry II in October 1171 launched a new phase of the conquest. By grants of land, the King encouraged his barons to gain control of most of Ireland, marking their advance with formidable castles. A justiciar or king's lieutenant was appointed to head a central government in Dublin. Irish parliaments were occasionally summoned, and from 1297 included elected representatives. However, Gaelic resistance to the Norman conquest was never wholly eliminated, and the foundations were laid for eight centuries of Anglo-Irish conflict.

THE FLIGHT OF THE EARLS

In September 1607 a French ship sailed from the northern harbour of Rathmullan in Lough Swilly. On board were Hugh O'Neill, Earl of Tyrone, and Rory O'Donnell, Earl of Tyrconnell, together with more than ninety of their family and followers. Their ship was bound for Spain, but fierce storms forced them to disembark in France in early October. Thereafter they made their way to Rome, where they remained in voluntary exile, and where O'Neill died in 1616.

For centuries the native Irish had struggled to preserve the Gaelic way of life, with its distinct laws and customs. Through inter-marriage many of the Norman conquerors had become "more Irish than the Irish", until the King of England's rule had been confined to a small area around Dublin known as the Pale. During the sixteenth century, successive Tudor monarchs tried to extend their authority, but there was always strong resistance from the northern province of Ulster. Religion became a factor in the struggle. Soon after the Protestant Queen Elizabeth came to the English throne in 1558, an Irish parliament passed an Act of Supremacy confirming her as head of the Irish Church, and requiring office-holders in church and state to swear allegiance to her. The Gaels and their "Old English" allies remained staunchly loyal to the Roman Catholic Church.

As a boy, Hugh O'Neill had been taken into the care of Elizabeth's viceroy, Sir Henry Sidney, and raised as an English nobleman. After returning to his native County Tyrone, he had shown his loyalty by helping to suppress the Desmond rebellion in Munster. In 1587 he was recognised as Earl of Tyrone, and was granted extensive territory under the Crown. A year later, however, he ignored a government order to execute survivors of the Spanish armada who landed in Ireland, and in Dublin there were increasing doubts about O'Neill's loyalty. The doubts were justified. O'Neill was allowed to keep 600 men in arms at the Queen's expense, and by regularly changing them he was able to train a substantial army. Lead to roof his new castle at Dungannon was turned into bullets.

Elsewhere in Ireland, English government was tightening its grip. In Connacht, the Gaelic lords had submitted to the Crown. In Munster, following the defeat of the second Desmond rebellion in 1583, English settlers had acquired confiscated land. In Ulster,

though, there were no English settlers or garrisons west of Lough Neagh. With its mountains, lakes and forests, the region was eminently defensible, and O'Neill found a vigorous ally in Red Hugh O'Donnell of Tyrconnell, who had escaped from imprisonment in Dublin. In 1593, O'Neill took the now illegal Gaelic title of "The O'Neill" and prepared to lead the Ulster chiefs in defence of territory and religion.

O'Neill was a skilful commander, and his troops exploited the difficult terrain to harry the English columns. In 1595, he won a handsome victory at Clontibret, near Monaghan, over an army commanded by his brother-in-law, Sir Henry Bagenal. Bagenal was to lose his life during the Battle of the Yellow Ford, on the River Blackwater, in 1598. This was O'Neill's greatest triumph. In 1601 he made the mistake of marching to the southern port of Kinsale to join an invading Spanish army, and the Irish were routed in unfamiliar country.

O'Donnell fled to Spain, but O'Neill returned to Tyrone. In 1603 he submitted to the Queen's representative, Lord Mountjoy, as O'Donnell's brother Rory had earlier done. However, despite a generous settlement in which he retained his earldom, O'Neill found English rule unacceptable. When the flight of the earls denuded Ulster of its Gaelic aristocracy in 1607, the government took the opportunity to confiscate six of the nine Ulster counties. The subsequent plantation of Ulster, introducing Protestant settlers from England and Scotland, laid the foundation of today's divided island.

THE CURSE OF CROMWELL

On 15 August 1649 Oliver Cromwell landed at Ringsend, near Dublin, with an army of 3,000 battle-hardened Ironsides. The civil war in England had ended, and King Charles I had been executed seven months earlier. In Ireland, however, the Roman Catholics had been in revolt since 1641 and held much of the island. They had generally taken the King's side, though some had seen in England's turmoil a chance to restore Irish independence. Cromwell entered Dublin as "lord lieutenant and general for the parliament of England". A fanatical Protestant, he intended to offer no quarter to papist rebels who had massacred English and Scottish settlers. In Ireland, he could use confiscated land to pay off debts to his troops and to the so-called "Adventurers" who had financed the parliamentary cause.

From Dublin Cromwell marched north to Drogheda, which was defended by an English Catholic and royalist, Sir Arthur Aston. When his surrender demand was ignored, Cromwell stormed the city and ordered the death of every man in the garrison, describing this as "a righteous judgment of God upon these barbarous wretches". The nearby garrisons of Dundalk and Trim took flight. Having secured the route to Ulster, Cromwell turned on the south-eastern port of Wexford, this time slaughtering townspeople and garrison alike. Neighbouring towns quickly submitted.

Cromwell's campaign ended with an assault on Clonmel where, after stout resistance, the defenders withdrew by night. In May 1650 he returned to England, leaving his son-in-law, Henry Ireton, in command. Within two years Catholic resistance was at an end. Many Irish soldiers were allowed to seek their fortunes in Europe. Catholic land-owners were largely dispossessed, but some were given the option of settling on less fertile land in Connacht. Cromwell himself had been in Ireland a mere nine months, but his brutality left an indelible impression on the native Irish. "The curse of Cromwell on you" became an Irish oath.

The rebellion of 1641 had made an equal impression on the Protestant settlers in Ulster. The plantation of Ulster had been entrusted to three classes of land-owner. From England and Scotland came "undertakers", who were required to bring in their tenants. Secondly, there were "servitors", who had served the Crown in Ireland, and who were allowed to take Irish tenants as well as newcomers. Finally, some native Irish were allowed to own land, if they were deemed trustworthy and agreed to adopt English farming practices. In the event, too few immigrants were attracted to Ireland, and the undertakers found they had to accept Irish tenants. This intermingling of the two religious groups was to prove a dangerous cocktail.

The worsening conflict between King and parliament in England encouraged the native Irish to seek to recapture their forfeited lands. They were also impelled by a fear that if the

Puritans triumphed in England, the Catholic religion would be suppressed. On 23 October 1641 a series of uprisings in Ulster spread panic among the Protestant settlers. Those who were not killed by the rebels fled for safety into the defended towns, where plague and starvation soon took their toll. Modern historians suggest that first accounts of the rebellion exaggerated the number of deaths and the extent of atrocities committed by the native Irish. Wherever the truth lies, the rebellion created in Protestant minds a distrust of their Catholic neighbours which has survived to modern times.

The hostilities gradually spread throughout Ireland, and in 1642 a Catholic government was formed in Kilkenny. The rebels found an experienced commander in Owen Roe O'Neill, nephew of Hugh O'Neill, who won a famous victory at Benburb in 1646. However, the Catholic cause was always prone to internal dissension, and O'Neill died before he could test his generalship against Cromwell.

THE BATTLE OF THE BOYNE

No date in Irish history is better known than 1690. No Irish battle is more famous than William III's victory over James II at the River Boyne, a few miles west of Drogheda. James, a Roman Catholic, had lost the throne of England in the bloodless "Glorious Revolution" of 1688. William was Prince of Orange, a Dutch-speaking Protestant married to James's daughter Mary, and became king at the request of parliament. James sought refuge with his old ally, Louis XIV of France, who saw an opportunity to strike at William through Ireland. He provided French officers and arms for James, who landed at Kinsale in March 1689. The lord deputy, the Earl of Tyrconnell, was a Catholic loyal to James, and his Irish army controlled most of the island. James quickly summoned a parliament, largely Catholic, which proceeded to repeal the legislation under which Protestant settlers had acquired land.

During the rule of Tyrconnell, the first Catholic viceroy since the Reformation, Protestants had seen their influence eroded in the army, in the courts and in civil government. Only in Ulster did they offer effective resistance. In September 1688, while James was still king, apprentice boys in Londonderry closed the city's gates to deny admission to a Catholic regiment under Lord Antrim. In April 1689, the city refused to surrender to James's army, and survived the hardships of a three-month siege before relief came by sea. The Protestants of Enniskillen defended their walled city with equal vigour, and won a number of victories over Catholic troops. Eventually, James withdrew from the northern province.

William could not ignore the threat from Ireland. In August 1689 Marshal Schomberg landed at Bangor with 20,000 troops and, with Ulster secure, pushed south as far as Dundalk. James's army blocked further progress towards Dublin, but there was no battle and the two armies withdrew to winter quarters. In March 1690 the Jacobite army was strengthened by 7,000 French regulars, but Louis demanded over 5,000 Irish troops in return. The Williamites were reinforced by Danish mercenaries and by English and Dutch regiments. When William himself landed at Carrickfergus on 14 June, he was able to muster an army of 36,000 men. He began the march towards Dublin. There was some resistance near Newry, but the Jacobites soon withdrew to the south bank of the River Boyne.

The battle was fought on 1 July 1690 at a fordable river bend four miles west of Drogheda. The main body of Williamite infantry was concentrated on fording the river at the village of Oldbridge, which was approached by a deep and sheltering glen. First, however, a detachment of cavalry and infantry made a flanking attack upstream, which forced James to divert troops to prevent his retreat being cut off. William's army was stronger by at least 10,000 men, but after these troops were drawn off he had three-to-one superiority in the main arena. By mid-afternoon the Jacobite army was in retreat, outpaced by James himself, who rode to Dublin to warn the city of William's approach. He was in France before the month was out. On 6 July William entered Dublin, where he gave thanks for victory in Christ Church Cathedral.

The Battle of the Boyne is recalled each July in the celebrations of the Orange Order, not on the first day but on "the Twelfth", for eleven days were lost with the change from the Julian to the Gregorian calendar in 1752. It was not the end of the Williamite campaign, and the King had returned to England before the Dutch general Ginkel's victory at Aughrim and the final Irish surrender after the siege of Limerick in 1691. The Treaty of Limerick was not ungenerous to the defeated Catholics, but they were soon to suffer from penal laws designed to reinforce Protestant ascendancy throughout Irish life.

GRATTAN'S PARLIAMENT

For most of the eighteenth century, the Irish parliament in Dublin was prepared to accept a subordinate role. In return, England would always defend Protestant interests in Ireland. Under Poynings' Law, passed in the fifteenth century, no Irish act could pass without the approval of the king and his advisers in England. The viceroy in Dublin Castle was a member of the British government. In 1720, a Westminster act known as "the Sixth of George I" gave the British parliament the right to pass laws for Ireland. The only weapon of the Irish house of commons, now wholly Protestant and largely controlled by wealthy landlords, was its powers of taxation.

Irish agriculture was generally inefficient, and manufacturing trades suffered from restrictions imposed to protect English merchants. British policies were challenged by writers such as Jonathan Swift, Bishop George Berkeley and Charles Lucas, founder of the *Freeman's Journal*. Within the Irish parliament itself, a reforming group known as "patriots" eventually emerged, led by Henry Flood and the Earl of Charlemont. They believed that a more representative assembly would, while preserving the Protestant interest, achieve more for Irish commerce.

In 1775 Flood accepted a government post, and leadership of the patriots passed to Henry Grattan, a young lawyer whom Charlemont had brought into parliament. With the outbreak of rebellion in the American colonies, followed by French and Spanish intervention, Britain was forced to withdraw troops from Ireland. Fears of a French invasion led to the formation of a Protestant militia, the Volunteers. Charlemont became their leader, and the Volunteers threw themselves behind the demands for reform. Bending to Grattan's oratory, a fearful government removed most of the trade restrictions in 1779, and in 1782 Irish parliamentary independence was conceded. Westminster repealed the 1720 act, and the Irish parliament removed the most oppressive parts of Poynings' Law.

"Grattan's parliament" is the name usually given to the two decades of parliamentary independence which ended with the Act of Union in 1800. Certainly, there was much celebration in 1782, and parliament voted its hero £50,000 in gratitude. The final years of the century saw great commercial activity, and a prosperous Dublin acquired many of the handsome Georgian buildings for which it is noted today. However, Grattan soon faced a challenge from the embittered Flood, now out of office, who questioned Grattan's achievement and forced a further Renunciation Act from Westminster in 1783. In November 1783, a Volunteer convention in Dublin drew up a plan for parliamentary reform which Flood presented as a bill. It was immediately rejected by the Irish parliament, whose members refused to be coerced by an armed assembly, and the convention dispersed. The unity of the "Protestant nation" had been destroyed, and the Volunteer movement gradually disintegrated.

To its credit, the Irish parliament eased the penal laws, and in 1793 Catholics gained the right to vote. However, a property qualification restricted the franchise, and the bulk of seats were still controlled by a few wealthy Protestants. Nor were Catholics allowed to sit as MPs. It was a fundamentally unstable position, given that the population was overwhelmingly Catholic, and far-sighted Protestants began to consider that their ascendancy could only be maintained in a United Kingdom of Great Britain and Ireland. The rebellion of the United Irishmen in 1798 convinced the government of the need for change. When its first Bill of Union was rejected by the Irish house of commons, the government embarked on a cynical programme of bribery, buying votes with offers of titles, government posts and compensation. In 1800, dressed in Volunteer uniform, an ailing Grattan begged the commons not to agree to the Union. For once his oratory was in vain, and parliament voted itself out of existence.

THE 1798 RISING

The Society of United Irishmen was founded in Belfast in 1791. Its inspiration was a young Dublin lawyer, Theobald Wolfe Tone, who was invited to Ulster after publishing a pamphlet entitled "An argument on behalf of the Catholics of Ireland". Northern Presbyterians also suffered from religious discrimination, though less severely, and had absorbed republican ideas from the American and French revolutions. With the formation of a Dublin society, pressure for reform grew, and relief acts were passed in 1792 and 1793. However, Tone sought revolution rather than reform, and hoped for French help in severing the link with Great Britain. After Britain and France went to war in 1793, the United Irishmen came under increasing pressure from the government. Tone chose exile in America in preference to being prosecuted for treason, and the United Irishmen evolved into a secret society bound by revolutionary oaths.

Returning to Europe in 1796, Tone persuaded the French to invade Ireland, but bad weather prevented a landing. Despite this setback, the United Irishmen continued to recruit members, particularly among disaffected Catholic peasants. Meanwhile, the government had passed an act providing for harsh measures against those who held illegal arms or administered illegal oaths. An army under General Lake conducted an oppressive campaign to disarm Ulster, seen as the most dangerous province. The government had many informers among the United Irishmen, and in March 1798 most of the Leinster leaders were arrested in Dublin. The only leader of the United Irishmen with military experience, Lord Edward Fitzgerald, was captured on 19 May, four days before the date fixed for the rising.

Apart from some short-lived but bloody skirmishes in towns and villages west of Dublin, the rising was confined to the northern counties of Antrim and Down, and to County Wexford. The Wexford rising, which began on 26 May, was a spontaneous and frightened response to the cruel measures of magistrates searching for arms and conspirators, but the rebels in turn committed acts of great savagery. They found a remarkable leader in Father John Murphy of Boolavogue, who quickly assembled an army of Catholic peasants equipped with muskets and pikes. The few troops were outnumbered and poorly led, and the rebels soon commanded most of the county. The government was slow to react, but the rebels' attempts to spread the rising to neighbouring counties were halted by defeats at Arklow and New Ross. On 21 June, General Lake stormed the rebel headquarters at Vinegar Hill, near Enniscorthy, and resistance soon ended. Murphy was later captured and executed.

In Ulster, where the rebels were mainly Presbyterians, the rising began later and was soon over. On 7 June, some 3,000 men attacked the garrison in Antrim town. An informer had revealed their plans, however, and reinforcements soon arrived to scatter the rebels, who fled to their homes. Their leader, Henry Joy McCracken, was captured and hanged. In County Down the rising came to an end on 13 June, when the United Irishmen were defeated at Ballynahinch. Their leader, Henry Monroe, was also hanged.

Meanwhile, Wolfe Tone had persuaded the French government to send another expedition to Ireland, but it sailed from La Rochelle long after the rising had been defeated. On 23 August, 1,000 French troops under General Humbert landed at Killala Bay in Connacht. Local peasants swarmed to his banner; however, after an early victory at Castlebar, he surrendered on 8 September to the superior army of the Marquis Cornwallis, who had been appointed lord lieutenant and commander-in-chief in anticipation of a rising. Tone himself was captured in October aboard a French ship in Lough Swilly. Court-martialled in Dublin, he pleaded for a soldier's death before a firing squad, but was sentenced to be hanged. He committed suicide in prison on 19 November 1798.

Catholic Emancipation

The Union of Great Britain and Ireland came into effect on 1 January 1801. In future Ireland would have one hundred MPs in the British house of commons, as well as twenty-eight elected peers and four Protestant bishops in the house of lords. Catholics were still prevented from sitting in parliament, and indeed were excluded from many public offices. Cornwallis, as lord lieutenant, had pressed for Catholic emancipation to be included in the terms of the Union which the two parliaments were asked to agree. However, the British prime minister, William Pitt, was persuaded that this might be unacceptable to the Protestant MPs in Dublin.

Pitt believed that emancipation would make the Union acceptable to Irish Catholics and planned to put the necessary legislation before the enlarged Westminster parliament. The Catholic hierarchy in Ireland consequently supported the Union. However, there were many opponents at Westminster, in addition to most of the new Irish MPs. More important, King George III was implacably hostile to emancipation. When Pitt found his own cabinet divided on the issue, he resigned in February 1801.

In the aftermath of the 1798 rising, the issue of emancipation was not of great consequence to the mass of Catholics. However, the Catholic hierarchy and upper classes, as well as the growing numbers of Catholics in commerce and the professions, felt some sense of betrayal. The issue continued to receive attention at Westminster, where Henry Grattan made it his principal concern, but a number of reforming measures were rejected.

The turning point came in 1823, when Daniel O'Connell founded the Catholic Association. O'Connell, born into a prosperous Catholic family in County Kerry, had been educated in France until forced out by revolutionaries. In Ireland, where he became a successful barrister, he was critical of the 1798 rising and of the agrarian violence perpetrated by secret societies such as the Whiteboys and Ribbonmen. By pursuing peaceful methods, and by mobilising Catholic smallholders and workers in mass demonstrations, he came to dominate Irish politics for two decades.

The Catholic Association sought not only to remove what remained of the penal laws, but also to further Catholics' interests at a time when many were suffering from economic depression and from unsympathetic landlords. When an annual membership fee of one guinea proved unpopular, O'Connell introduced a "Catholic rent" of one penny per month, and numbers soared as the money was collected by parish priests. Although opposed to violence, O'Connell never hesitated to speak aggressively in depicting Catholic grievances. The government responded, first by trying to prosecute him, then by banning the association, but O'Connell was undeterred.

At the 1826 general election, pro-emancipation candidates won several seats. The most notable success was in County Waterford, where O'Connell's oratory roused the so-called "forty shilling freeholders" to vote against a member of the powerful Beresford family, who owned much of the county. In 1828, O'Connell himself won a by-election in County Clare. Unable to swear the oath of supremacy, O'Connell could not take his seat, but the victory persuaded the government led by the Duke of Wellington that emancipation must be granted.

King George IV reluctantly yielded, and early in 1829 a Catholic Relief Bill received royal assent. Henceforth Catholics could sit in parliament without taking the oath of supremacy, and almost every office was open to them. However, the forty-shillings franchise was raised to ten pounds, so that many of O'Connell's supporters immediately lost their vote. O'Connell became an influential MP at Westminster, but failed in his second major campaign. In 1840 he formed an association to press for repeal of the Union, but lost authority after he yielded to a government ban on a proposed mass meeting at Clontarf in 1843.

THE GREAT FAMINE

I n 1800, some five million people lived in Ireland. By the
autumn of 1845, when the Great Famine struck Ireland, there
were more than eight million. Many of them were wretchedly
poor, eking out a precarious living on tiny plots of land, and
dependent on each year's potato crop. Hunger was no novelty to
peasant families, for there had been partial failures of the potato
crop in other years. However, these had always been of limited
duration, and confined to a small number of counties. The Great
Famine lasted from 1845 to 1848, and crop failure affected the
whole island.

The cause of the famine was a fungus disease which caused the
potato plants to rot in the ground, giving off an appalling stench.
The blight first destroyed crops on the eastern seaboard of America
in 1842, then appeared in England in the summer of 1845. In
September, the counties of Wexford and Waterford reported the
disease. More than half the Irish potato crop failed in 1845. Sir
Robert Peel, the British prime minister, appointed a commission
to investigate the problem, but scientists were unable to explain
the disease, let alone find a cure. In 1846, the potato crop was
a total failure.

Peel, to his credit, also introduced relief measures. In November 1845, the government spent £100,000 on buying grain from America, in the hope of keeping food prices down in Ireland. He appointed a relief commission which set about forming local committees to raise money and to distribute food. At Westminster, in part prompted by Ireland's problems, Peel succeeded in repealing the protectionist corn laws in June 1846. This opened up the prospect of cheap imports from America. A month later he was out of office, defeated over a bill to deal with the growing agrarian disturbances in Ireland.

The new Whig government, led by Lord John Russell, believed in a free market and was content to leave the supply of food to private merchants. However, the Irish peasants were unused to a cash economy, for they had traditionally worked for a landlord in return for a plot of land on which to grow potatoes. The government hoped that Irish landlords would bear the major responsibility for their tenants' welfare, but many landlords already faced ruin. The most successful relief came from soup kitchens, originally set up by bodies such as the Society of Friends. Where public works continued, they were often delayed by bureaucratic procedures, and workers' health suffered from the inadequacy of wages to buy what food was available. Evictions were common.

Even the weather contributed to the distress, for the winter of 1846–47 was exceptionally cold and wet. To starvation was added typhus and relapsing fever, both commonly called "famine fever". Scurvy and dysentery flourished, and in 1849 an outbreak of

cholera claimed many lives, particularly in the larger towns. Many sought to escape to America, only to drown at sea in over-crowded "coffin ships". Those who did reach the New World were often weakened beyond recovery.

Eventually the government reformed the poor law system, so that outdoor relief was added to the limited accommodation of the workhouses. Medical services were improved with the establishment of temporary fever hospitals. By the end of 1849, the potato blight had passed and crops returned to normal. About one million people had died, and another million had emigrated. The population continued to decline, not only through emigration but through later marriages, lower birth rates and an end of the sub-division of farms which had made Ireland so vulnerable to crop failure. The famine was to prove a watershed in Anglo-Irish relations, for the inadequacy of government measures left an enduring legacy of bitterness in Ireland and among those thousands of Irish emigrants who found a new life across the Atlantic.

The Fenian Movement

In 1848, a small group of revolutionaries known as Young Ireland launched an ill-prepared uprising which was quickly quelled. Among them were James Stephens and John O'Mahony, who both sought refuge in Paris, a city which harboured plotters exiled from many countries. In 1853, O'Mahony sailed to America in the hope of encouraging Irish emigrants to support a new rising. Stephens returned to Ireland in 1856, tramping throughout the country to assess the people's mood. On 17 March 1858, he formed in Dublin the secret society which became known as the Irish Republican Brotherhood. Later in the year he sailed to America, where O'Mahony became leader of a new organisation called the Fenian Brotherhood. It took its name from the *fian* or band of warriors led by the legendary Gaelic hero, Finn Mac Cool, and the name Fenians came to be used for the whole body of revolutionary conspirators.

The Fenian movement, which sought a revolution "sooner or never", quickly attracted thousands of young supporters. When one of the 1848 rebels, Terence Bellew McManus, died in America in 1861, his enormous funeral procession through Cork and Dublin showed how widespread was the sympathy for the Young Ireland ideas which Fenianism now embodied. However, Stephens came in conflict with other nationalist organisations which sought to end the Union by constitutional methods, and the Catholic Church was generally hostile. In 1863 his decision to found a weekly newspaper, the *Irish People*, was criticised by O'Mahony, who preferred secrecy.

Fenianism was strongly supported by Irish emigrants in America. Many gained military experience in the American Civil War, and when this ended in April 1865 Stephens promised an Irish rising later in the year. However, the government had been alerted by its spies, and in September the *Irish People* was suppressed. Stephens and his closest associates were arrested, but he escaped from prison and reached America. The government quickly took the offensive, arresting suspects and confiscating arms. Some army units, thought to include Fenian sympathisers, were moved from Ireland.

Stephens had now lost influence, and it was left to civil war veterans, notably Thomas Kelly, to instigate a rising in March 1867. It was no more effective than the 1848 fiasco. Kelly had made his headquarters in England, where Fenianism had strong support among Irish emigrants, and had earlier failed in an attack on Chester Castle to capture arms and ammunition. He and another Fenian were arrested in Manchester on 11 September. A week later, they were rescued while being taken from court to gaol. A police officer was shot dead, and three Fenians were subsequently hanged for his murder. They became known as the Manchester martyrs, and their words from the dock, "God save Ireland", were soon embodied in a popular patriotic ballad.

Other Fenian prisoners were treated more leniently, with death sentences being commuted. However, the execution of the Manchester martyrs, for what was perceived as an accidental killing, aroused great anger among Irish people at home and abroad. Equally, there was a growth of anti-Irish feeling in England, particularly in December 1867, when a number of Londoners were killed or severely injured when a Fenian bomb exploded during a rescue attempt at Clerkenwell prison.

Almost fifty years would pass before the next rising in Ireland, and during this period the main thrust of Irish nationalism was provided by a parliamentary campaign for home rule. However, the Irish Republican Brotherhood preserved the ideal of total separation from Great Britain, and some Fenians were active in new organisations like the Land League and the Gaelic League. Of more immediate importance, though, the Fenian rising had further persuaded some British politicians that the Irish problem called for radical measures. Among them was a future prime minister, William Ewart Gladstone.

HOME RULE

William Ewart Gladstone became British prime minister in 1868. "My mission is to pacify Ireland", he immediately affirmed. Among his first measures was the disestablishment of the Church of Ireland, a recognition that it was inappropriate to have a formal link between the state and a denomination supported only by a small minority of the Irish people. His Land Act of 1870 gave greater security to some tenants, and those who left their holdings could claim compensation for improvements they had made. However, the act proved unsatisfactory in practice, and agitation for land reform steadily increased. Equally important was the demand for home rule.

In 1870 Isaac Butt, a Protestant lawyer who had represented Fenian prisoners and campaigned for an amnesty, founded the Home Government Association. He initially envisaged a Dublin parliament responsible for domestic affairs, with Irish MPs continuing to sit at Westminster. The association was replaced in 1873 by a more aggressive Home Rule League, and after the following year's general election (the first with a secret ballot) fifty-nine MPs were committed to home rule. Butt died in 1879, and after a further general election in 1880, the Irish parliamentary party (now sixty-one in number) elected Charles Stewart Parnell as its leader. During the next decade he dominated Irish affairs as Daniel O'Connell had once done.

Parnell, a wealthy Protestant land-owner from County Wicklow, might have seemed an unlikely advocate of home rule. However, his American mother had always been hostile to England, and he himself was horrified by the execution of the Manchester martyrs. Soon after entering parliament, he shocked the house of commons by saying, "I never shall believe any murder was committed at Manchester." He quickly adopted the obstructionist tactics initiated by his fellow MP, the Fenian Joseph Biggar, exploiting parliament's rules of procedure to delay business and force the government to attend to Irish grievances.

Parnell's militancy found favour among such Fenian leaders as Michael Davitt, founder of the Land League, and John Devoy, who was active in America. The Fenians were still committed to the use of physical force, and there were many agrarian outrages during the "land war". However, Parnell's support for land reform was valuable, and the three men formed a loose alliance known as the "New Departure". Parnell became president of the Land League, but he was dissatisfied with Gladstone's Land Act of 1881 and his provocative language resulted in imprisonment in Dublin and suppression of the league. Seven months later, secret negotiations led to his release, and to new legislation which helped tenants with arrears of rent.

A new organisation, the Irish National League, switched the emphasis to home rule. After the 1885 election the eighty-six members of Parnell's party held the balance of power at Westminster, and Gladstone introduced his first Home Rule Bill. Ninety-three of Gladstone's own Liberal MPs voted against the bill, and it was defeated.   In 1889 Parnell was cited as co-respondent in a divorce case, and the scandal cost him the leadership of his party.   Two years later he was dead.

The struggle for home rule continued, and Gladstone introduced a second bill in 1893, only to see it defeated in the house of lords. However, the Liberal Party was now firmly committed on the issue, and after the 1906 general election enjoyed a huge majority in the house of commons.   The Parliament Act of 1911 reduced the peers' veto on legislation to a delaying power.   A new Home Rule Bill was introduced in 1912, was rejected by the lords, and became law in 1914.   With the outbreak of the First World War in August 1914 it was agreed that this Government of Ireland Act should not be implemented until the war was over – but by 1918 much had changed.

"Ulster Will Fight"

Within Ireland, the strongest opposition to home rule came from the Protestants of Ulster. They formed a majority in the northern province, but a minority within the island. The 1641 rebellion had induced a siege mentality which was reinforced during the struggle between William of Orange and James II. Secret societies, agrarian crime and faction fighting became common in the eighteenth century, with Protestant Peep o' Day Boys pitted against Catholic Defenders. In 1795, a pitched battle in County Armagh led to the formation of the Orange Order, which soon mustered enormous support among Protestant labourers and small farmers. In 1798, reports of sectarian atrocities in County Wexford confirmed most northern Protestants, even those who had risen in Antrim and Down, in a distrustful hostility towards Catholics.

Since the Union, Ulster had become much more prosperous than the other provinces. Tenant farmers had greater security than elsewhere, had a valuable cash crop in flax, and escaped the worst of the potato famine. Industry flourished, and Belfast was a thriving port. However, after Catholic emancipation, it was apparent that Protestants would be in a minority in any all-Ireland parliament.

When Gladstone introduced his Home Rule Bill in 1886, his Conservative opponents formed a political alliance with the Ulster Protestants which was to last almost a century. "The Orange card was the one to play", wrote a leading Conservative, Lord Randolph Churchill, who also coined the watchword "Ulster will fight, and Ulster will be right." The bill was greeted by severe rioting in Belfast. Sectarian violence was no novelty in the city, but the 1886 riots were the worst the city had seen. There were further disturbances in 1893, in response to Gladstone's second bill.

The Ulster Unionist Council was formed in 1905, linking the Orange Order and Unionist associations throughout the province. It marked their determination to keep the province within the Union, even if Protestants in the rest of Ireland were ultimately forced to yield to nationalist aspirations. In 1910, Irish Unionism gained a new leader in Sir Edward Carson, an eminent barrister and MP for Dublin University. Carson was prepared to defy the British government and parliament. In 1911, he told a large rally on the outskirts of Belfast to prepare to take over the government of Ulster if a Home Rule Bill passed. On 28 September 1912, he was among almost half a million men and women who signed a "solemn league and covenant" pledging themselves to use "all means which may be found necessary to defeat the present conspiracy to set up a home rule parliament in Ireland".

In 1913, the Ulster Unionist Council announced the formation of the Ulster Volunteer Force. Some military drilling had already begun, and before long 90,000 men had been recruited under the command of Sir George Richardson, a distinguished soldier. They were poorly equipped until the council commissioned a Belfast businessman, Major Fred Crawford, to purchase arms secretly in Germany. In April 1914, 35,000 rifles and five million rounds of ammunition were smuggled into Larne Harbour and swiftly distributed throughout the province.

With home-rule legislation in abeyance during the First World War, members of the Ulster Volunteer Force formed the 36th (Ulster) Division, suffering heavy casualties at the battle of the Somme in 1916. In 1920, a new Government of Ireland Act provided for a separate Northern Ireland parliament covering six counties with a Protestant majority. The 1920 Act was never fully implemented, and in 1922 the parliament in Belfast exercised its right to exclude Northern Ireland from the newly created Irish Free State, and to remain part of the United Kingdom. The partition of Ireland, so long implicit in the contrast between Ulster and the rest of the island, became a reality.

THE EASTER RISING

On 24 April 1916, Patrick Pearse stood outside the General Post Office in Dublin and read a proclamation announcing the establishment of an Irish republic under a provisional government. Among the seven signatories of the proclamation was James Connolly, head of the para-military Irish Citizen Army, who had earlier led a successful occupation of the building. Elsewhere in Dublin, armed men had taken over key points such as the Four Courts, the College of Surgeons overlooking St Stephen's Green, and Boland's Mills. It was Easter Monday, and there were few people in the centre of Dublin to witness the rising. Many army officers had gone to the Fairyhouse races.

Almost all the revolutionary leaders were members of the secret Irish Republican Brotherhood. The outbreak of war had persuaded them that in England's difficulties lay Ireland's opportunity. As earlier rebels had looked to France for help, they now turned to Germany, which promised to send arms. In addition to the small Irish Citizen Army, formed in 1913 to defend workers against police harassment, there were thousands of Irish Volunteers, a body formed in response to the Ulster Volunteer Force. Like the UVF, the Volunteers carried out a successful gun-running exploit, landing arms at Howth, near Dublin, a few days before war was declared.

The Volunteers had been infiltrated by members of the IRB, which had secretly fixed Easter Sunday as the date for the rising. The Volunteers' leader, Eoin MacNeill, only discovered the plan on 20 April. Two days later, he learned that a German ship bringing arms had been scuttled. Realising that a rising was doomed to failure, he cancelled all Volunteer manoeuvres. Despite this setback, and knowing that their forces would be limited to a modest number of Dublin Volunteers as well as the ICA, Pearse and Connolly decided that a rising must take place, if only as a blood sacrifice to arouse the Irish people.

Once the rebels had occupied some of their targeted buildings, they had nowhere to go. The rest of Ireland showed little disposition to join the rising, apart from a few minor outbreaks of violence, and in Dublin there were few recruits. The government, which had not expected a rising, responded quickly by declaring martial law. The army in Dublin was reinforced, and heavy artillery was deployed against the republican strongholds. On Friday, General Sir John Maxwell arrived from England to assume overall command, and made it clear that he would not hesitate to destroy every building held by the rebels. The GPO, headquarters of the rebels, was soon in flames. On Saturday afternoon, Pearse agreed to Maxwell's demand for unconditional surrender.

In different circumstances the rebels might have been treated more mercifully, but Britain was at war, and the army and police

had suffered greater casualties than Pearse's men. Ireland was still under martial law, and Maxwell was at liberty to inflict retribution. On 3 May, just four days after the surrender, a terse announcement was made that Pearse and two other signatories of the republican proclamation had been tried by court martial and shot. By 12 May the total of executions had reached fifteen, including Connolly and the three other signatories. Another seventy-five rebels had the death penalty commuted to penal servitude, including Countess Constance Markievicz, who would later become the first woman elected to the Westminster parliament.

In halting the executions, the government was responding to a wave of public revulsion, but the damage had been done. Ireland had a new gallery of martyrs, and earlier apathy or even hostility towards republicanism was replaced by sympathy for the independence cause. Of some 3,400 arrested following the surrender, more than half were imprisoned or interned in England, where they plotted a new onslaught on British rule.

INDEPENDENCE

The principal beneficiary of the 1916 rising was Sinn Féin (Ourselves Alone), a political movement founded in 1905 by Arthur Griffith. Griffith, who opposed the use of force, argued that the Irish MPs should quit Westminster, set up their own assembly in Dublin, and make British government unworkable. As public opinion turned against the Irish parliamentary party, Sinn Féin won several by-elections in 1917. Among its successful candidates was Eamon de Valera, who had fought in 1916, and he soon succeeded Griffith as president of Sinn Féin. When a general election was held in December 1918, Sinn Féin won seventy-three of the 105 Irish seats, most of the rest going to the Unionists.

Many of the successful Sinn Féin candidates were in prison in England. However, on 21 January 1919 twenty-five members met in Dublin as Dáil Éireann (Assembly of Ireland) and adopted a declaration of Irish independence committing themselves to the republic which had been declared in 1916. On the same day, the War of Independence began when two policemen were killed by Volunteers in County Tipperary as they guarded a consignment of gelignite. The Volunteers, who now became known as the Irish

Republican Army, continued to arm themselves through attacks on police barracks and army depots.

The principal figure in the IRA was Michael Collins, who had fought in the GPO in 1916. Collins built up a formidable intelligence network, together with a special squad which assassinated British intelligence officers and key Irish detectives. Elsewhere, men like Ernie O'Malley and Tom Barry perfected guerilla tactics, with mobile "flying columns" that carried out surprise raids. In 1920 the British government reinforced the Irish police with ex-soldiers known as Black and Tans, wearing a mixture of police and army uniforms, and later with ex-officers known as Auxiliaries. Atrocities were committed by both sides and much property was destroyed, including many country houses owned by Anglo-Irish gentry.

By 1920 the British government, led by David Lloyd George, was prepared to seek a compromise which would keep Ireland within the British Empire but make concessions to Irish nationalism. A new Government of Ireland Act provided for a measure of home rule to be exercised by two parliaments in Ireland, and in a general election unopposed Sinn Féin candidates took all but four seats in "Southern Ireland". Since Sinn Féin was unwilling to enter the new Dublin parliament, Lloyd George offered de Valera negotiations on the future of Ireland. The two sides agreed on a truce, and on 11 July 1921 the War of Independence ended.

Later in the month, when de Valera met Lloyd George in London, he refused to accept the terms offered by the British prime minister. When the second Dáil met in August it elected de Valera president, and thereafter negotiations with the British government were conducted by a delegation led by Arthur Griffith. On 6 December 1921, after protracted discussions and faced with Lloyd George's threat to resume hostilities in Ireland, the weary delegates agreed to a treaty providing for an "Irish Free State" with dominion status, and allowing the six counties of Northern Ireland to remain within the United Kingdom.

The treaty also provided for an oath of allegiance to the crown, which de Valera refused to accept. When in January 1922 the Dáil approved the treaty by sixty-four votes to fifty-seven, he ceded the presidency to Griffith. Collins was appointed head of a provisional government. Though unhappy with the treaty, he rightly believed it opened the way to greater freedom and independence, and his views were substantially endorsed in a general election. De Valera still refused to accept the treaty, however, and the inauguration of the Irish Free State was marked by a civil war which lasted until the anti-treaty republicans conceded defeat in May 1923.

MODERN IRELAND

Ireland's troubled history continues. The centuries-old division between Protestant and Catholic, between planter and Gael, finds expression in the partition of the island. Northern Ireland has remained part of the United Kingdom, while the Irish Free State further distanced itself by becoming the Republic of Ireland in 1949 and ceasing to be part of the British Commonwealth of Nations. Within Northern Ireland, Protestants and Catholics have never reached more than an uneasy accommodation. In 1972 continued civil strife led the British government to abolish the parliament and government of Northern Ireland, and to create a Northern Ireland Office as unrepresentative of those it governed as Dublin Castle once was. Both the United Kingdom and the Republic of Ireland are members of the European Community, but participation in this multi-national venture has yet to make Ireland's two "tribes" more at home with one another. Nor has the Anglo-Irish Agreement of 1985, which gave the Irish government a weighty consultative role in Northern Ireland affairs, effected the reconciliation it sought. The Irish problem remains unsolved. There may be lessons to learn from history that would alleviate the persistent troubles – but, if so, who is willing to learn them?